SWITCHED ON, FLUSHED DOWN, TOSSED OUT

Investigating the Hidden Workings of Your Home

Switched On, Flushed Down, Tossed Out

INVESTIGATING THE HIDDEN WORKINGS OF YOUR HOME

BY TRUDEE ROMANEK

ART BY STEPHEN MACEACHERN

Annick Press
Toronto • New York • Vancouver

There are some strange things going on in our house.

My folks claim it's nothing special. They're so blind. Just because stuff like electricity, water, and heat has been coming into our home for years, they don't think twice about it. But I say, how exactly does it happen? And what about all the stuff that goes OUT of our house? How does it get out, and just where does it go? And this stuff doesn't just happen at our house. Other people report the same things in their homes too.
It's one big giant mystery.

But not to me! I'm positive that there must be a huge network of agents — clever undercover spies — who make sure all of this happens according to plan. At least, I'm pretty sure there's a network. And, okay, I don't know exactly what the plan is ... but I'm SURE agents are behind these mysterious happenings. How else could these happenings happen? I just don't have all the information I need to prove it. But I'm going to find out everything!
This is Special Investigator Casey officially launching ... Operation Discovery!
Note to Myself: I will need to investigate thoroughly ALL suspicious activities I read about in books, newspapers, and other sources. They may provide clues about the very case files I'm investigating!

Contents

I've noted the areas in my own home and at my friend Taylor's that need investigation. They are as follows:

TROUBLED WATERS

FACTS:
Every single time I turn a faucet, water pours out. This morning the water coming from our kitchen tap smelled v-e-r-y strange.

QUESTIONS:
Where exactly does this water come from? How do agents deliver clean water to us at any moment? What is that smell?

MY THEORY:
Special water agents must have built top secret passages to carry rain to our homes. Maybe when one of those agents was checking our passage, she spilled something into it. Maybe THAT'S what I can smell!

What you're smelling is chlorine gas. It kills germs that may be in the water.

Take a look around your city or town. See a lake anywhere nearby? Or maybe a river? Your water probably comes from there. Or it may come from a well or an aquifer, a stream or lake that's deep underground. But before any of it reaches your tap, stuff has to happen to it.

Water specialists pump lake or river water through a filter. That gets rid of any leaves or garbage that might be floating in it. Then the specialists test that lake water, or water they're pumping up from underground, to see exactly what's in it. Not all water's clean enough to make it into your kitchen. Some contains germs that would make you sick if you swallowed them. The water specialists add chemicals, such as chlorine, to kill those germs and make the water safe for drinking.

The clean water usually gets pumped into large storage tanks. Look around the place where you live. You might see a storage tank standing up on tall legs. If it's near your home, the water pouring out of your tap probably comes from there.

NEWS

ICE COLD

People in some parts of the world have melted glaciers coming out of their taps. About 40% of the tap water in Boulder, Colorado, used to be ice in the Arapahoe Glacier above the city.

Others too have realized that melted ice can be good to drink. Companies that sell water in bottles have started harvesting water from glaciers and icebergs. Desert countries have even considered towing a giant iceberg to their area so that as it melts, they'll have fresh water. So far, no one's figured out how to get the iceberg where they want it without it melting too fast or shattering.

Are giant icebergs sub-zero spy bases for international operations?

DANGEROUS JOURNEY

FACTS:
It seems that cleaning systems at the water treatment plant get rid of any germs. BUT—the water must leave the safety of the storage tanks to travel the treacherous path to our house.

QUESTIONS:
What journey does the water take to get to our sink? Could germs infiltrate somewhere on that journey?

MY THEORY:
As the water travels from the storage tanks to our taps, especially sneaky germs could slip in through any openings along the way. Unless the agents have created a counterplan …

Openings along the way? There are some, but germs would have a tough time getting in through them. You see, the water comes charging downhill toward your home. If there are any openings, the water rushes OUT. Nothing could push its way IN.

The water storage tanks are up on tall legs or inside a high hill. That's so that when the water leaves the tank, gravity will pull it down, like water over the lip of a waterfall.

Large pipes lead out of the storage tanks. Those pipes split up like tree branches into many smaller and smaller pipes. Each one carries water to one house or other building nearby. Gravity forces the water down into the pipes so that every pipe is full of water, all of it pushing forward, trying to get out.

One of those pipes brings water to your home. Then that pipe divides into more pipes. One carries water to your kitchen, another one carries it to your bathroom, and another leads to your laundry room. Under the floor or behind the walls, where you can't see it, your bathroom pipe divides again. This new batch of smaller pipes takes water to the sink, toilet, and bathtub. Every one of those pipes is full of water that's being pushed by all the water behind it.

Then you come along. One little twist of the tap and *sploosh!* Water pours out. Immediately, more water from the pipes and the high water tank rushes in to take its place.

Drip, Drip, Drop

You've turned the tap off as hard as you can and a drip still leaks out! Taps are hollow tubes, like the pipes that carry water to them. Near the end of the tube, though, is a wall with a small hole in it. That hole is where the water flows out.

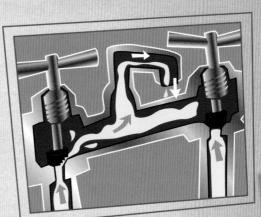

Near the hole is a stopper that's just the right shape to plug up the hole. When you turn the tap off, the stopper moves into the hole, blocking the water. But if the stopper is a little crooked or doesn't fit as tightly as it should, water squeezes through the tiny openings around it and plops into the sink below.

Agents should upgrade equipment.

UPHILL CLIMB

FACTS:
My friend Taylor lives in an apartment up on the 12th floor. Water gets to their taps too, but sometimes not as much comes out.

QUESTIONS:
If water comes through pipes underground to get to our homes, how does it get from there up to the 12th floor? Why does less water come out sometimes?

MY THEORY:
Maybe apartment buildings aren't hooked to the underground pipes like our house is. Maybe they get their water from somewhere else. Maybe Mrs. Griffith, the landlady, is working with agents in the building to take some of the water and use it to power an ingenious spy machine that decodes messages and relays them to master spy command in the center of the earth ... Or maybe not.

There goes the water pressure again.

Somebody downstairs must be taking a show...

Hey, Casey. It's your roll.

Tall buildings use pumps to help water reach the top floors.

Modern high-rise buildings have strong pumps in the basement or on the ground floor. Water coming in from the city pipes passes through one of these pumps. That gives the water an extra push along its way. It's that push that forces the water in the pipes all the way up to the top floors. The taller the building is, the bigger a pump it needs to do the job.

Many tall apartments and office towers have an extra water pipe that brings water in to a sprinkler system. If there's ever a fire, the sprinklers on the ceiling of each story open and the water sprays out to help put out the flames. And when the firefighters get there, they can attach their hoses to one of these pipes to get extra water to fight the fire inside the building.

Since the water comes up from the basement, water reaches the lower taps first. If they are turned on, then there's less water being pushed on up to the other floors.

Are "builders" special agents?

Welcome to the Empire State Building!

EARLY WATER SUPPLY SYSTEM

In 1930, builders in New York City had to find a way to get water to go straight up, against gravity. They were constructing the Empire State Building. At 381 m (1,250 feet) tall, it was the tallest building in the world at that time. Water rushing into its basement pipes would have to go uphill to get to all 102 stories of the building. There was no way it could make it up there on its own!

So, the builders installed giant steel water tanks at six different levels of the tall tower. Pumps in the basement sent water up to fill those tanks. Then, when a tap was turned on, the water could easily flow down to it from a tank above.

Well, Mrs. Griffith, your pump is getting old. That's why it's not pumping the water up to all 12 floors as well as it used to.

Are the giant water tanks *Top* secret water sources?

The Water Works
Case file #4

IN HOT WATER

FACTS:
Turning one tap makes cold water rush out of the faucet, but turning the other brings hot water OUT OF THE VERY SAME FAUCET!

QUESTIONS:
What heats the water? What stops the hot water in the pipe from heating up the cold water that's there too?

MY THEORY:
Perhaps agents have miniature laboratories hidden under every kitchen and bathroom sink! The steam given off by secret experiments conducted there might be what heats the water.

So, you're sure you've never noticed any tiny test tubes under the sink?

No test tubes. I'm sure. *This* is what heats up our water.

Some of the cold water that comes into your house or apartment heads for your hot water tank. That tank might be in the basement of your house or high-rise building or in a closet of your apartment.

Every water heater has a thermostat. That's a dial where you can set just how hot you want your water to get. Cold water comes into the tank at the bottom. There, behind a metal wall, electric elements or flames from burning gas or oil heat the water to the temperature set on the thermostat. As the water heats up, it gets lighter and floats up above the heavier cold water. A pipe leads from the top of the heater and divides up to connect to all the hot water taps in your home.

When you turn on one of those taps, hot water comes out. Sometimes it's cool at first. That's because that water has been sitting in the pipe between the tap and the hot water tank. Since there's no flame there to heat it, it gradually cools down. Behind that cooler water comes hotter stuff, fresh from the tank.

As the water flows out of the tap and the pipe, more cold water rushes into the bottom of the hot water tank to be heated.

Taps that have just one spout are connected to a cold water pipe *and* a hot water pipe. Water from both mixes together. When you turn or push the single handle or each of the two handles, you can change how much of the water coming out is cold and how much is hot.

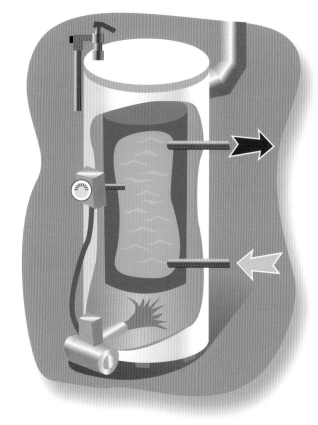

DO-IT-YOURSELF HOME REPAIRS

TOO MUCH WATER

Not all water comes into your home through a pipe. Sometimes rainwater or melting snow seeps through tiny holes and gaps in the roof or gets in through spaces around windows and doors. If there's a lot of it, it could trickle down inside the walls and soak through, making a soggy mess inside your home.

Cracks in the basement floor or walls often let water from the ground seep through, especially if heavy rains have flooded the soil around the house. Many homes have a sump pump. It sits in a hole in the basement. Since the hole is lower, water seeps in there first. As water fills the hole, it triggers the sump pump to turn on and pump the water through a pipe that leads outside, away from your house.

Perimeter NOT secure!

OUTGOING EVIDENCE

FACTS:
When I shower or wash my hands, the water, soap, and all the dirt and slime they washed off just disappears down the drain.

QUESTIONS:
Where does it go? How do the agents dispose of this gross stuff?

MY THEORY:
Agents have built ANOTHER set of hidden passages that lead from the drains in our sinks straight down to the center of the earth. There, the heat from all that molten rock boils the water and stuff clean and turns it into steam. Then, uh, then that steam comes shooting out of volcanoes when they erupt! ... I think.

Remember to wash your hair, Casey. And scrub really well behind your ears to get all the old skin off.

Cool agency gadget! Agents exercised while they got clean!

Museum of

See a replica Stool Shower and other fascinating artifacts in our new exhibit, 19th-century Life.

SIT-AND-SPRAY
Ever had a shower sitting down? One of the earliest household showers invented was the American Virginia Stool Shower of the 1830s. This wooden contraption sat in a bathtub of water. To use it, you would sit on its stool and use its hand pump to pump the bathwater up the pipe and out the sprayer. With your foot you controlled a pedal that moved the scrub brush up and down to scrub your back.

Every home has an "in" pipe that brings fresh water in and an "out" pipe, called the drainpipe, that takes used water out. The water from your kitchen sink, your bathtub, your dishwasher, even your toilet, all gets whisked away from your home through this drainpipe.

Outside, your drainpipe and the drainpipes of all your neighbors connect to large underground pipes called sewers. These carry everyone's waste water to the sewage treatment plant. There, the water passes through a screen that catches any large objects that have been flushed. As the flowing water heads inside a first tank, it slows down and any sand in it falls to the bottom of the tank.

The water goes into other tanks, where chemicals and bacteria – tiny creatures too small to see without a microscope – clean it. The chemicals remove some materials that would make lakes and rivers unhealthy. The bacteria eat the dirt, old skin, and other unhealthy bits floating in the water and poop out harmless waste. These helpful bacteria also eat other bacteria, like the ones from human poop, that could make people sick.

Finally, the water swirls around tall tubes that give off ultraviolet light. The light kills any dangerous germs that might still be in the water.

Once the used water is clean enough, it flows out of the treatment plant through more pipes into a lake or river, sometimes far from the community. The water has to be properly cleaned so it won't make the nearby people, animals, and plants sick.

At least that's how that water specialist explained it when she was here.

POOP PROCESSING

FACTS:
When I flush the toilet, a whole lot more than water disappears.

QUESTIONS:
Where does all the guck go? How do agents deal with that smelly mess undetected?

MY THEORY:
The guck disappears to some spy location. After all, no one ever talks about where it goes. Maybe if I send a recording device along the same path, I could infiltrate that secret location and get clues.

WIPING UP

Before people could buy toilet paper in stores, they wiped their behinds with all sorts of things, including sand, leaves, rope, and just their hands. In North America corn husks were a popular choice. In Japan people used seaweed.

When you flush the toilet, water floods the bowl and washes your body's "leftovers" – urine (that's pee) and feces (that's poop) – out of your house, into the sewers, and on to the sewage treatment plant.

While the watery part travels through to a separate tank to get cleaned, the solids settle down to the bottom of their own treatment tank. This guck is called sludge. There are tiny bacteria, like the ones that cleaned the water, in the sludge tank too. They eagerly gobble up the sludge.

What's left over is called "biosolids" – a black liquid that hardly smells at all. In many communities farmers use the biosolids from the sewage plant to fertilize their land, just as they might use cow or pig manure.

Houses in the country and in some villages often don't have a treatment plant. Instead, pipes carry their waste to an underground sealed pit called a septic tank. Inside it, the solid waste rots, or decomposes. The left-over liquid drains into an underground pit, where it gets cleaner as it seeps further down through sand or gravel.

It's kind of gross to think about where this mess goes, but somebody has to look after it or your town would be a smelly, unhealthy place to live.

Solid waste settles to bottom of first tank.

Water travels to second tank for cleaning.

Do-It-Yourself Home Repairs

Plumbing

Maintenance

SMELL TRAP

One flush isn't enough to get the stinky stuff in your toilet all the way to the treatment plant. Instead, it hangs around in the sewer pipe. If it wasn't for that bendy part underneath the toilet and the bend under your sink too, smells of your body's left-overs — and other people's too — could waft up through those drain-pipes into your home.

The bend in the pipe is called a trap because it traps some water in it. The water blocks the smells from get-ting into your home. Thank goodness!

Heating

Cooling/Heat Pumps

Insulati

Built-in security feature!

CURBSIDE DROP-OFF

FACTS:
Sanitation workers pick up stuff from my house regularly.

QUESTIONS:
Is our garbage like clues or evidence? What do they do with it?

MY THEORY:
Sanitation workers are agents in disguise. By analyzing the garbage, they piece together the lives of each person in the neighborhood. That way they can decide which ones are clever and stealthy enough to become part of the agency. (I hope they saw the good mark I got on my last math test …)

Garbage – plastic wrap, used tissues, and soggy cereal – goes into a garbage can or bag. If you live in a town or city, your family probably hauls its garbage and recycling out to the curb. People who live in apartments can put their garbage and recycling into giant bins or down narrow chutes that lead to bins in the basement.

Workers in garbage trucks pick up your trash and take it to a landfill, or dump. But after they "dump" it there, other trucks bring in sand or dirt every day to spread over the garbage. That keeps it from blowing around or smelling too much while it slowly rots.

The trouble is it takes such a very long time to rot. Researchers who study garbage by digging through landfills have found 40-year-old lettuce and hotdogs that still haven't rotted. And since people throw out so much stuff – an average of nearly 2 kg (4½ pounds) per household each day – landfills all over the world are getting full. The less you send to the landfill, the better.

In the News

UP IN SMOKE

In some communities, garbage is burned in a big oven called an incinerator. The temperature inside the incinerator has to be just right, though, or the smoke coming out pollutes the air. Experts are trying to come up with other ways to get rid of trash.

Messages sent by smoke signal?

REASSIGNMENT

FACTS:
Not all our leftovers go to the dump. Some materials are picked up and recycled into something else.

QUESTIONS:
What makes these materials so important? Why does the agency spend time, energy, and money turning them into something new?

MY THEORY:
These materials are worth recycling because they contain valuable spy equipment hidden within the scrap metal, cardboard, and other junk.

Yeah, it can be valuable stuff. The city gets paid for aluminum and some other things by the factories that recycle them.

Paper, cardboard, and many containers made of metal, glass, and some plastics can be put into recycling bins.

A truck sort of like a garbage truck carries your recycling to a building where the paper, plastic, glass, and metal get sorted. Each different material goes to a separate factory where it's cleaned and melted or mulched to make new paper, new glass or plastic containers, and other items.

The more you recycle, the less you send to the landfill. But recycling is even more important for other reasons. Recycling old discarded paper, metal, and so on uses a lot less energy and water than creating new products from raw materials. Making paper from recycled paper uses between 30% and 50% less energy than making it from trees.

Recycling paper also means we cut down fewer trees and use less of other raw materials too. Every ton of recycled office paper means 380 gallons of oil saved. And the paper recycling process reduces the amount of pollution produced by 95%.

Recycling saves our resources, like trees, oil, and water, uses less energy, and creates less pollution.

RECYCLING FACTS

Did You Know?
● The energy saved by recycling a single glass bottle instead of creating a brand new one would light a 100-watt bulb for four hours.
● The energy saved by recycling one aluminum can instead of making a new one could keep your television running for three hours.
● Computer disks, carpet, paint, egg cartons, motor oil, park benches, and hundreds more products can be made from recycled materials. Many fleece jackets are made of recycled plastic bottles.

Make our community a better place to live! Reduce, reuse, and recycle every day!

Computer disks! Possible tracking of sensitive data!

OPERATION ORGANISM

FACTS:
We put our leftover fruit and vegetables in our compost bin. Mom says tiny organisms are at work in there. She gives the compost to Mr. Spiros for his garden.

QUESTIONS:
What sort of transformation takes place inside the compost bin? Is Mr. Spiros an agent growing vegetables as part of an experiment the agency is running?

MY THEORY:
The organisms in the compost bin may help Agent Spiros grow veggies that contain stuff to make agents faster and lighter so they'll be sneakier spies. Or they'll be good at ballet ...

Mr. Spiros! All this for us? I don't think you kept any for yourself!

Now, you take it. Without all that good compost of yours, they'd never grow so well.

Lots of food leftovers can be turned back into rich soil to feed gardens and lawns. It's called composting, and it's completely natural. All the forest floors and meadows on earth have been composting leaves, sticks, even dead animals for millions of years.

Rotting bananas, vegetable peels, eggshells, tea bags, and coffee grounds – people who compost dump all these scraps inside a large box or bin that sits outside in a sunny spot in the yard. They also add plain old dirt because it contains the secret ingredient: tiny creatures called microbes.

These creatures – mainly bacteria and fungi – are much too tiny to see without a microscope, but dirt is teeming with them. One gram (less than ¼ tsp.) of soil might contain one billion microbes – as many microbes as there are people living in China.

Microbes love to munch on the peels, stems, cores, and everything else in a compost bin. Every now and then the person composting stirs the mixture inside around. That lets in air and mixes the microbes around. Together they eat through the compost and poop out humus, a terrific food for growing plants.

Some communities provide a place for people to bring their compostable material. Then the community composts it and gives or sells it to gardeners.

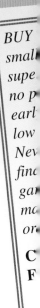

Red Wiggler: special agent code name??

Red wiggler worms by mail order.

CREEPY-CRAWLY COMPOSTERS

You can compost indoors if you've got the right kind of worms to help you. Red wiggler worms can live in a box of shredded newspaper somewhere in your home. Every so often you add fruit and veggie scraps and the worms will gobble them up. These worms poop out humus just like composting microbes do. And they work fast: every day, a red wiggler worm eats half its weight in scraps. If you weigh 36 kg (80 lbs.), that's like you eating 18 kg (40 lbs.) of food every day!

Last few left!

THE BEST EVER MINIATURE ROSE
BUSHES – only 6 inches tall.
If you are a passionate rose gardener then

SUPER POWER

FACTS:
Electric power runs all kinds of things we depend on, so it's important to keep power traveling to where it's needed.

QUESTIONS:
Who is in charge? Who lets the power flow to my house when I want it for something?

MY THEORY:
This transformer may be headquarters for the division of the agency that delivers power to the houses in my neighborhood. These power workers may really be agents. I wonder if they would teach me the secret agency handshake …

The storm blew a tree down on the transformer station. We'll have it up and running again shortly.

What exactly passes through this station?

Somewhere, maybe far away from your home, there's a place where electric power is made. It might be made when water pushes big turbines around, or when wind turns the blades of hundreds of windmills. The electric energy that's in your house might even have come from a nuclear power plant.

Electric power flows out of the power plant through heavy wires, then spreads out through other wires toward many houses and businesses, offices and stores, hospitals and schools. Like the endless stream of water that flows through your pipes, power followed by more power surges along the wires.

In some communities, the wires are all underground. In others, they are held high over your head by large wooden poles that line the roads and streets.

POWERLESS

✳✳✳✳✳✳

In August 2003, about 50 million people in northeastern North America discovered how much they depend on electricity. A huge power surge shut down hundreds of power stations in Ontario and New England that are connected in the North American Power Grid.

Suddenly, there were no traffic lights, no computers, no alarm systems, no working gas pumps, no restaurants, and no appliances to cook dinner on. In many buildings, elevators stopped working and people were stuck inside them for hours. Some people didn't even have water since theirs is pumped out of the ground using electric power.

Luckily, most of the problems were sorted out within 24 hours and life could get back to normal.

Stealth missions may have gone undetected.

Transformers change the high-voltage electricity that comes from generating stations to the lower-voltage electricity used in homes.

ZAPPED!

FACTS:
Electric energy is created at a power plant somewhere not far away. Electric energy powers many things inside our home — lights, computers, refrigerator, everything that plugs in.

QUESTIONS:
How does the electric power get to the lights and everything else? Who controls that part of the electrical journey?

MY THEORY:
Local agents keep an eye on every household, flipping a giant switch to let the power flow to a house when anyone inside heads for the television to turn it on.

Power comes into your home through two large wires . . .

Do you have a lamp in your room? Even when it's turned off, there's still electric energy in it. It's actually flowing all around your room, just waiting for someone to flick a switch and let it out.

The power comes into your home through two large wires that lead to a box with an electrical panel inside it. There, the power divides up and spreads out through the wires that lead to each room of your home. Some heads for lights on the ceiling, some powers the stove, still more heads for the outlets to wait.

If you plug in a lamp, electric energy flows into it right away, just waiting for you to flip the "on" switch. When you do, the energy rushes further inside, to the bulb, and then rushes back through a third large wire that leads out of the house and back to the transformer. That round trip – from transformer to bulb and back again – is called a circuit, and it's what lights the bulb.

The power is ready and waiting at each switch and outlet – waiting for you to flip the switch and complete the circuit. That's why touching an outlet can give you a dangerous shock: the power is already there.

FACT

FLASHING LIGHTS

The lights that are turned on in your home are actually flashing. Really! The electric energy that lights them flows back and forth, turning the lights on and off about 120 times every second. You just can't see the flickers because your eyes don't recognize changes that happen that fast — just like you can't see the separate frames in a motion picture movie.

PERFECT for sending messages undetected!!!

TUNING IN

FACTS:
Any time I flip on the television, there's a program to watch.

QUESTIONS:
How do pictures of people performing end up inside my TV? And my radio doesn't even plug in. Where does its music come from?

MY THEORY:
Agents who are experts in communications are ready at all times to pass along important messages and data hidden within TV and radio transmissions. (The commercials must contain VERY important information since they get repeated so often ...)

Laughter bursts from your television and pictures dance across its screen. How do these sounds and images get into your house? Some come right through the walls!

The show you're watching right now was recorded in a studio weeks ago! You can watch it today because a technician at a distant TV station is playing back the taped show. The station's equipment sends the show out of the station.

Some stations send shows out on radio waves – waves of invisible energy that travel through the air like ripples crossing a pond. Other stations have equipment that changes a digital, computerized version of the show into light waves – flashes and pulses of light. These light signals travel through cables made of thin strands of glass called optical fibers. Inside the fiber optic cables the light signals travel along by bouncing back and forth off the shiny, mirror-like surface inside.

Cable companies receive these shows and change them into digital signals – bits and bytes of computer information for digital television systems – and analog signals, which are pulses of electricity that regular TVs can receive. Cable companies send these shows out to neighbor-hoods through cables that are buried underground or hang from telephone poles. A thin cable branches off from the main cable, leads into your house behind the walls, and connects to your TV.

Your TV turns the bits and bytes or the pulses of electricity that come through the cable for each program into sound and the tiny shifting dots that go together to make up the moving, changing picture on your screen.

Space Sounds

Shows from radio stations don't need any cable to get to you. Their radio wave signals travel through the air and your walls too. Your radio "catches" the waves and translates them into music and voices.

Your radio catches other kinds of energy too. That crackling and hissing you hear as you tune in a radio station might be the electricity from lightning in a distant country. Some of it could even be radiation energy from a galaxy exploding far out in space.

Some TV signals get to your home through the air. If you don't have cable, your TV picks up whatever stations nearby transmit out on radio waves. And if you have satellite TV, the satellite dish outside your home picks up strong signals coming from a satellite orbiting the earth. Those signals originally came from stations further away. The dish sends those signals inside to your TV through a short wire of its own.

HEARING THINGS

FACTS:
Somehow my voice travels into my phone and out someone else's, even if they're halfway around the world.

QUESTIONS:
How does that happen? Who carries the messages through?

MY THEORY:
Outside every house is a tube leading from its telephone. The agency has trained hundreds of parrots to hide quietly, one outside each tube, waiting for the phone to be picked up. The parrot hears the number that's dialed and listens to the message. Then it flies to the house matching the phone number and repeats the message, imitating the caller's voice, in through the phone tube sticking out of that house!

So, Taylor, I guess our spy agency isn't controlling the TV, but I STILL think they're in charge of other stuff.

Like what?

Like ... (gasp!) telephone calls! Taylor, maybe the agency looks after the phone lines and uses them for important spy transmissions!

GETTING STARTED
GETTING YOUR COMPUTER ONLINE

The Internet is a lot like a telephone system for computers. It connects your computer with other, larger computers so that you can get the messages and website information stored there.

Telephone lines are great for carrying electrical pulses of sound. When you download something with more information, though, like a picture or a computer game, it could take a long time with the type of signals telephones normally use. Internet companies have created new systems for coding and sending these computer-bound signals. The information travels in larger amounts so your computer gets more of it faster.

So, operator, I'm hoping you can explain it to me.

Telephone exchange offices direct your calls to where they're supposed to go.

MUSEUM OF TECHNOLOGY
Pipeline Robots

Water and sewage isn't all that's in under-ground pipes. In some cities, these large pipes hold fiber optic cables that carry infor-mation, such as telephone calls and e-mails, from a citywide network of cables into each office building.

One company uses a robot named SAM (Sewer Access Module) to lay cables in sewer pipes. SAM has a camera to show technicians above-ground what's in the pipe. He's skinny enough to get inside pipes only 20 cm (8 in.) wide to fix cables or install new ones.

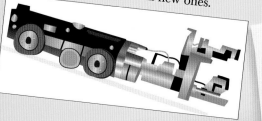

SAM has a camera. Perfect for spying!

When a friend phones you, you can hear every word she says. Her telephone changes the sounds of her voice into electrical signals. Those signals travel along a telephone cable out of her house to an underground or overhead phone line. That carries the signals to the local telephone exchange office and on, from exchange office to exchange office, until they reach the one in your community.

From there the signals head through another telephone line to your house, then in through telephone wires behind your walls and to your phone. Your telephone translates the signals back into her voice and sends it into your ear. *Voilà!* It's almost like your friend was standing right beside you.

Now people can talk on the telephone from their backyard, the grocery store, even from a boat. Cellular telephones, or cell phones, send the information through the air on radio waves.

If you live in the Arctic or another remote place where there are no telephone lines, it can be hard to contact the rest of the world. Satellite phones can help. They send radio wave signals up to a satellite in orbit above Earth. The satellite sends the signals back down to a phone system in a different part of the world. It's like throwing a ball and having someone catch it and pass it further on.

PIPING HOT

FACTS:
Dad says there's usually a fire in our basement. That fire is what heats our house.

QUESTIONS:
Why doesn't the fire burn our house down? What keeps the fire from going out? Why has our fire gone out now?

MY THEORY:
Maybe the agency isn't happy about my snooping and they've put our fire out!

Homes in cold places usually have equipment to heat them. Some homes have a boiler system. A boiler in the basement produces hot water. That water travels through pipes to metal radiators throughout the home that radiate, or give off, the heat.

Another type of heating system still used in some homes is electric baseboard heaters. Low heaters run along near the floor in each room. Electricity heats up the element inside, which gives off heat, kind of like the glowing element inside a toaster.

Many homes have a furnace in the basement. A heat source inside the furnace, with temperatures as high as 815°C (1500°F), heats the air. Then a fan blows that heated air out into rectangular tunnels made of metal. They're called ducts, and they lead under the floors and behind the walls to each room in your home. At the end of each duct is a narrow vent. That's where the warmed air comes out. Other larger vents – the ones your pennies and Lego pieces always fall into – pull cool air in and down through different ducts to the furnace to be warmed again.

Different furnaces heat the air in different ways. Electric furnaces use elements. Some fuel-burning furnaces burn heating oil or propane that gets pumped into a storage tank connected to your furnace. Many furnaces now burn natural gas that comes straight into your home through a pipe connected to the gas company. Gas pipes also bring in gas to fuel natural gas appliances – a gas clothes dryer, fireplace, or kitchen stove.

EARTH'S FURNACE

Some homes don't need a furnace. In places such as Iceland, Japan, Italy, New Zealand, and parts of the United States, many homes are warmed by geothermal heat — heat from Earth's blazing hot core.
Steam rising from deep cracks in the ground heats water, which then flows through pipes in homes and other buildings to heat them. Experts think Earth's core is about 6000°C (10,832°F), as hot as the surface of the sun.

Secret underground movement?

I'll call someone to fix it in the morning. Let's get you another blanket.

PLAYING IT COOL

There's your trouble. The burners wouldn't light, so your fuel couldn't burn. I just need to replace this.

That won't affect our air conditioning, will it? It's still okay?

FACTS:
Dad says the furnace and the air conditioning are connected somehow.

QUESTIONS:
What is air conditioning and how does it cool down our house?

MY THEORY:
Maybe air conditioning means that agents put giant blocks of ice in our ducts in summer to keep our home cool.

Linked to the "Cold War" my parents always talk about?

THAT'S COOL

What's the coldest place in your home? Your fridge. Foods such as meat, milk, and leftovers go bad really quickly if they're not put in the refrigerator. Before the refrigerator became popular in the early 1900s, people found another way to keep food cool and fresh. In winter, workers cut blocks of ice from frozen lakes and shipped them by train all over North America. The ice was stored in ice houses or underground and covered in sawdust to keep it frozen as long as possible.

Ice wagons carried the ice blocks around the streets of towns to sell. Most homes had an icebox, a wooden cupboard that was lined with tin or zinc to hold in the cold air. A block of ice went in the top space and food went down below. The cool air from the ice would flow down around the food to cool it.

Many people who live in places that get hot have a central air conditioner, connected to their furnace, that makes cool air, a little like your refrigerator does.

The pipes inside an air conditioner are full of Freon. Freon evaporates, or turns from a liquid to a gas, just like moisture evaporates off your skin when you come out of the water.

Think of how cool your skin feels as the breeze blows by, making that water evaporate. As it evaporates into the air, it absorbs heat from your arm and takes it along. When Freon evaporates, it absorbs heat from whatever is around it, just like water does.

Part of an air conditioner

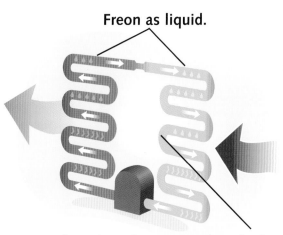

Freon as liquid.

Freon turns from liquid to gas and cools the air.

makes the Freon evaporate over and over again inside the pipes. As it evaporates, it takes heat from the air around it, making that air cold. Then the furnace fan blows that cold air into the home through the same ducts that carry warm air in winter.

Some homes have a newer kind of system called a heat pump. In winter, it pulls in every little bit of heat from the outside air and ground to heat your home. In summer, it pumps the heat *out* of your home.

SPECIAL EXHIBITION

You lost a lot of heat pretty fast. You might want to make sure there's enough insulation in your attic. That'll help your furnace AND your air conditioner.

INSIDE JOB

FACTS:
The furnace blows hot air. The air conditioner makes cold air. The furnace repair guy says insulation helps both.

QUESTIONS:
What is insulation? What does it do? How can it help keep the house hot AND cold?

MY THEORY:
Must be some new, top secret material. Maybe it can morph from a heat-producing cloth to a cold-producing cloth. (I wonder if it could warm up cold pizza ...)

This stuff's hardly top secret. Pretty well every home around here has some. It keeps what's inside in and what's outside out.

Heat stealers in disguise!

COLD FIRE

Some fireplaces can actually make your home colder. When a fire is crackling away, it spreads warm air into your home, but some warm air also rises up and escapes out the chimney. That air gets replaced by cold air that's sucked in through any tiny cracks around doors and windows. If it's a small fire, just starting or fading out, the cold air it's pulling into your home might be more than the warm air it's creating.

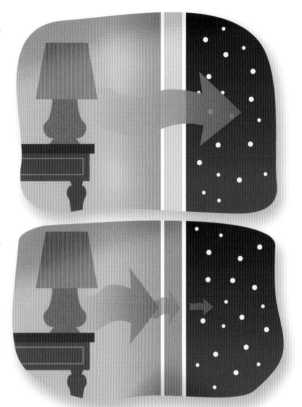

Heat loss without insulation.

Heat loss with insulation.

Your home and other buildings too are a little like your own body. You've got heat, but if you go out on a cold day, your heat flows away from you into the air. The same is true for your home.

The heat from your furnace spreads through your house and slowly makes its way through the walls and roof to the outside. Insulation is a layer of foam or puffy padding inside the walls and in the attic. It acts like a sweater, keeping the heat inside your home longer. Insulation keeps cool air-conditioned air inside longer too, the same way a padded lunch bag keeps your lunch cool longer.

There are other ways for heat or cool air to escape from your home. Leave a window open in winter and the heat will escape in no time. Air can even pass through any small gaps around loose-fitting windows or doors. Windows that close tightly and rubbery strips called weatherstripping that seal up gaps around doors keep air from slipping out or coming in. They're like the mitts and scarves of your home.

Casey, just what are all these questions about, anyway?

And what are you writing in that thing?

DO-IT-YOURSELF HOME REPAIRS

OUTGOING AIR

When your clean, wet clothes tumble around inside a dryer, hot air mixes with them, picking up some of the water still in the cloth and blowing it out the dryer vent. That vent leads right out of the building, carrying the hot air and water outside.

Air leaves your house through other vents too. A fan in the ceiling of many bathrooms blows air outside through a vent, taking bathroom smells and steam from the shower with it. Furnaces and fireplaces have vents or chimneys to carry harmful gases out of the home or apartment building.

special escape routes?

RECYCLED WATER?

At Healthy House in Toronto, Canada, all the water used in the house is rain or melted snow. It's collected from the roof, cleaned, and stored in an underground tank until someone turns on the tap. Waste water from sinks, showers, and the washing machine (but not the toilets) doesn't just slurp down the drain either. Instead it's cleaned and reused to flush toilets, take showers, and wash clothes. One day your home may work the same way.

In some communities, the waste water that leaves all the houses gets used again. It goes to the sewage treatment plant, where it gets partially cleaned. It's not clean enough to drink or even wash with, but it's good enough for other uses. Farmers can safely water their fields with it, and special trucks spray it on some city streets to clean them. Factories also use it in production.

In Singapore, there's very little fresh water for drinking. So, researchers have developed a treatment system to make water from the sewers clean enough to — gulp! — drink. They call it Newater. The country is also looking into ways of taking the salt out of sea water to make it drinkable.

BEYOND THE BOWL

Not all toilets are the same. Companies in Japan have developed toilets that glow in the dark or that will automatically lift their lid when you walk in the room. Some have nozzles that spray water on your behind to wash it.

As for what's inside the bowl, future toilets may analyze your urine (pee). The toilet seat will also measure your blood pressure and the toilet will send all that health information directly to your doctor.

Toilets may one day be able to suck the poop smells out along with the water. Or they may simply burn what you flush into a pile of ashes.

HOT AND COLD

Some people in Taos, New Mexico, don't worry about air conditioning or home heating. They've built special homes called Earthships.

Each Earthship has a wall of windows that faces south. The windows are angled so that less sun shines in during the hot summer months (when the sun is higher overhead) and more shines in to heat the home in winter (when the sun is down closer to the horizon).

Garbage Gas

Rotting garbage makes gas. The methane gas it gives off as it rots is bad for the environment, but it can also be a source of energy. Gas from landfill sites can be piped to generators and burned to create electricity. In Illinois, the Antioch Community High School gets almost all of its heat and power from gas generated by a nearby landfill.

In the United States alone there are 350 landfill sites fitted with pipelines and equipment to collect landfill gas and change it to power for nearby communities or factories. Another 600 American landfills could begin providing gas in the future – enough to power 1 million homes each year.

ENERGY FROM THE SUN

The electricity coming to your home may change too. One day energy from the sun — solar energy — may be collected by special satellites and beamed straight down to your house to do everything from lighting your lights to powering your computer.

FRIDGE WITH A BRAIN?

One day a computer in your refrigerator may be able to read the black and white lines of the bar codes on your food. Using that information, it will be able to tell you what foods are past their expiry dates and should be thrown out. It will also recognize what foods you've run out of. Then it'll send an e-mail to your favorite grocery store to order more.

POOP POWER

Astronauts on long missions have two problems: too much waste and not enough electrical power. NASA thinks it may have found a way to solve both problems.

Researchers are creating a new kind of fuel cell, or battery, that contains special microbes that love to eat poop and food leftovers. As they gobble up the astronauts' waste, the tiny creatures create energy from it that can be turned into extra electricity the spacecraft can use.

Who knows? One day these bacteria may create power on Earth from your poop too!

OUT OF THIS WORLD

High above Earth in the International Space Station, there's no gravity to pull water down through the pipes to a tap. Luckily for the astronauts working there, a system of fans and pumps pushes and pulls the water along through the station's pipes to get it where it needs to go.

Astronauts can't just turn on a tap to get a drink, either. Instead, the drinking water is stored in sealed bags. Hook the bag up to a dispenser, select the amount you want, and press a button. The dispenser pushes out just the amount you set it for.

"SMART" HOUSES

Imagine a house that knows you're tired and need a bath — and starts the water for you before you even get home. Or how would you like a house that turns off one light when you leave a room and turns on another in the room where you're headed?

Some companies are already building these smart houses. Sensors in the house can keep track of your movements and tell the computer where you are. You can also program into the computer the water temperature you like best in your bath, and when your weekly soccer game (or whatever) is finished, your perfect bath will be waiting.

FURTHER READING

The Water Works

Brimner, Larry Dane. *Glaciers*. True Book Series. New York: Scholastic Library Publishing, 2000. (Age Level 7–10)

Frew, Katherine. *Plumber*. Great Jobs Series. Danbury, CT: Children's Press, 2004. (Age Level 9–12)

Macaulay, David. *Unbuilding*. Boston: Houghton Mifflin Company, 1986. (Age Level 10–14)[1]

Waste Management

Lavies, Bianca. *Compost Critters*. New York: Dutton Books, 1993. (Age Level 5–8)

Goodman, Susan E. *The Truth About Poop*. New York: Penguin USA, 2004. (Age Level 7–9)

Brunelle, Lynn. *Bacteria*. Discovery Channel School Science Series. Milwaukee, WI: Gareth Stevens Publishing, 2003. (Age Level 9–12)

The Powers That Be

Schanzer, Rosalyn. *How Ben Franklin Stole the Lightning*. New York: William Morrow & Company, 2002. (Age Level 6–12)

Lauw, Darlene, and Lim Cheng Puay. *Electricity*. Science Alive! Series. New York: Crabtree Publishing Company, 2001. (Age Level 7–12)

Overcamp, David. *Electrician*. Great Jobs Series. Danbury, CT: Children's Press, 2004. (Age Level 9–12)

The Messengers

Worland, Gayle, and Jonathan Winter. *Radio*. Fact Finders Series. Mankato, MN: Capstone Press, 2003. (Age Level 7–10)

Durrett, Deanne. *Alexander Graham Bell*. Inventors and Creators Series. Stamford: Gale Group, 2002. (Age Level 8–10)

Mattern, Joanne. *Telephones*. Transportation and Communication Series. Berkeley Heights, NJ: Enslow Publishers, 2002. (Age Level 8–10)

Nobleman, Marc Tyler. *Television*. Fact Finders Series. Mankato, MN: Capstone Press, 2004. (Age Level 8–12)

Gearhart, Sarah. *Turning Point Inventions: Telephone*. Turning Point Inventions Series. New York: Simon and Schuster, 1999. (Age Level 9–12)

The Heat

Lauw, Darlene, and Lim Cheng Puay. *Heat*. Science Alive! Series. New York: Crabtree Publishing Company, 2001. (Age Level 7–12)

Snedden, Robert. *Technology in the Time of Ancient Rome*. Technology in the Time of Series. Chicago: Raintree Publishers, 1998. (Age Level 8–11)

Agents of Tomorrow

Romanek, Trudee. *Technology Book for Girls and Other Advanced Beings*. Toronto: Kids Can Press, 2001. (Age Level 8–11)

Tambini, Michael. *Future*. Revised Edition. Eyewitness Series. New York: DK Publishing, 2004. (Age Level 9–12)

[1] Describes the structure of the Empire State Building; a fictional account of how it would be demolished.

INDEX

Italicized numbers refer to illustrations.

We acknowledge the support of the Canada Council for the Arts, the Ontario Arts Council, and the Government of Canada through the Book Publishing Industry Development Program (BPIDP) for our publishing activities.

Cataloging in Publication

Romanek, Trudee

Switched on, flushed down, tossed out : investigating the hidden workings of your home / written by Trudee Romanek ; art by Stephen MacEachern.

Includes bibliographical references and index.

ISBN 1-55037-903-8 (bound).—ISBN 1-55037-902-X (pbk.)

1. Domestic engineering—Juvenile literature. 2. Dwellings—Electrical equipment—Juvenile literature. 3. Refuse and refuse disposal—Juvenile literature. I. MacEachern, Stephen II. Title.

TH6010.R64 2005   643   C2004-907002-9

The images in this book are drawn in ink, scanned into the computer, and color is added using Adobe Photoshop® software. The technical images are created using Adobe Illustrator® software.

Distributed in Canada by:
Firefly Books Ltd.
66 Leek Crescent
Richmond Hill, ON
L4B 1H1

Published in the U.S.A. by
Annick Press (U.S.) Ltd.
Distributed in the U.S.A. by:
Firefly Books (U.S.) Inc.
P.O. Box 1338
Ellicott Station
Buffalo, NY 14205

Printed in China.

Visit us at: www.annickpress.com

Acknowledgments
My sincere thanks to the following experts who guided and assisted me in my search for information: George Robinson and Dan Clark of Rogers Communications; Bill Beaty, Research Engineer at the University of Washington; Patrick Walsh of the University of Wisconsin's Department of Biological Systems Engineering; Barry Day of Day and Behn, Environmental Engineers; Ruth Yole, Environmental Waste Manager, Barrie, Ontario; Ralph Deshevy and Dave Truax of Barrie's Water Pollution Control Centre; Mark Cady, Inside Technical Consultant at Lennox Industries, Texas; and Ben Oakes of S. A. Armstrong.

Special thanks are due to Bob Argue for taking the time to review the manuscript and for his helpful comments. And finally, I'm grateful for the support of Annick Press, the creativity of Stephen MacEachern, and for the editing and enthusiasm of David Wichman.

To Rob with love, for the drains unclogged, taps installed, attics vented, electrical lines "fished," circuits rewired, and many other displays of household magic.
　　—T.R.

To Mom & Dad, thanks for teaching me how things work.
　　—S.M.